If

A

Fish

If A Fish
© George Burns and Cathexis Northwest Press

No part of this book may be reproduced without written permission of the
publisher or author, except in reviews and articles.

First Printing: 2020

Paperback ISBN: 978-1-952869-10-5

Cover art by C. M. Tollefson
Designed and edited by C. M. Tollefson

Cathexis Northwest Press

cathexisnorthwestpress.com

Cathexis Northwest Press

If

A

Fish

POEMS BY

GEORGE BURNS

Like Before, But Farther

If a Fish	13
Directions	15
I apologize for not writing a poem,	16
Imagining Flight	18
Tell Me,	20
Some Days	21
Let Us Resume Our Conversation	22
Another Ark	23

For a Steward in the Merchant Marine

Conjugations	27
First Flight	28
Puzzle	29
For a Steward in the Merchant Marine	30
What We Had in Our Hands	31
Bruised, I Guess	34
Sailor at Sea	35
My Gift	36
In the Revisions	37

Summer Light, Seattle

Momma's Boy	41
Broken Ice	42
Blackberries	44
Momma's Henchmen	45
Bleeder	47
Debut	48
1958	50
Partly Heliotropic	52
Forgiveness	54
The Flags of My Allegiance	55
Summer Light, Seattle	56
French Press	57

Love letter then,

The Coupe de Ville and the Burro	61
Plants in Tough Places	62
Wild and Windy Day	63
Elliptical	64
Hills Gathered Around Hecker Pass	65
The Meeting	66
Moon-Called	68
Bryce Canyon	70
how is it	71
On Making it to the Moon	72
It is	73
Love letter then,	74
Safety	75
Cricket Lover	76
Kilcatherine Remaians	77
Escrow	78
One Good Day	79
A Lesser Heaven	80
Autumnal Road	81
Another Flower	82
Bradley, Population 128	83
In Newgrange	84
Old Man's Love Song	85
Lost	86
Balloons	87
Old Address Book	88
Disconnected	89
Michigan	90
On the Amtrak	91
Sophisticated	92

Does the Road

I will leave behind	95
What We Hold	97
Inalienable	98
Treasure	99
Does the Road	100
The Wooden Box My Father Brought Back from Japan	101
Road's End	102
Writing Place	103

Like Before, But Farther

If a Fish

If a fish were to wiggle
out of the sea,
walk to my door,
stand on its hind fins,
ring the bell,
walk right on in,
drip sea water and
drop shimmering fish scales
onto my carpet, then

tell me,
in my mother tongue,
what it had practiced for years
in the sea's cold, deep heart
to say,

I would listen
to its every word,
but

if that fish came
all this way
and only gaped, wordless,
on my living room rug
the way fish gape
when they're fishes out of water,

I might be tempted
to hit it on the head
with a hammer,
or call the newspaper,
or return him quickly
to the sea.

And if that fish
still has some message
amid the coral and scattered bones
at the bottom of the sea
and cannot imagine how,
but still wiggles
and shimmers and flits,

not this place,
not this place,

then it is like a man
wanting his first wife
to hear something:
that he was a good father,
that he tried,
that he would like her
respect, if not her love,

and his whole life is like that—
never at the when and where
he's supposed to be at,
wiggling and twisting
some message.

A fish,
no tongue,
no feet,
no air,
only some stammering
across the table

at the bottom
of the sea.

Directions

Go past the light
to the top of the hill.

The next light
will be green, or red.
Believe the green.

Go right
all the way to the stop sign.

Go left
two blocks
to my street.

Go right,
count:
one, two, three.

That's me.
Come up my drive.

All the way to the top, my love.
Just like before, but farther.

I apologize for not writing a poem,

for keeping my talent
buried in a sock drawer,
for not listening,

for not knowing what you want to hear,
for thinking too much about what that might be,
for not even knowing what I want to say
until after it's said and even then—
well, what can words really say?

For plucking things out of thin air,
for picking green blackberries and imagining sugar,
for exaggerating in ways that no one understands,
for getting off-track because the grass was so inviting,

I apologize—
I'm doing the best I can
in the short amount of time
I've got.

I apologize for thinking we're different,
for thinking we're alike,
for thinking whenever I lose you, I lose myself—
for thinking whenever I lose myself, I lose you, too,

for thinking that being lost
in this blank white space
right in the middle of the page
is lonely.

I apologize for my loneliness and
for thinking you might know
this loneliness too,
for bringing you into this space on the page,
for thinking that if we met here, somehow,
I wouldn't have to apologize,

and this blank white space
would become
a rippling sea, and we,

white pelicans abobbing,
our wings rising and
pushing—lifting off.

Imagining Flight

The ancestors of birds
                theropods
        were small
                bipedal
                        reptiles
Arboreal
        they just let go
                                leaping
                                with outspread hands
                                        from branch
                                                        to branch
225 million years ago
                they became lighter
                        and lighter
Eventually
                just as we can see
                                the rising
                        and falling
                                of the hills
                                        they could see
                                        the mountains and rivers
                                                        of the winds
Flying
        they could go anywhere
                        Their reaching hands
                                became wings
                        and to support
the structure of wings
                                                their shoulders moved
Their sternum became
                keel-like
                to breast the heavens
                                and to enclose
                                a heart that wanted to fly
To glide, float and soar
                their bones
                        became hollow
                                honeycombed
                                        filled with air

Inside the wing-bones of large soaring birds
      lakes of blue sky
            islands of cumulus

Tell me,

now that it's April,
whisper in my ear some
apple-blossomed word.

Whisper it on pink-padded feet
past the sleeping cat.

A team of words,
traced and reined with vines
ringing little white bells.

Or, now that I'm sixty,
some small broken,
black rock of a word:

Tell me of the silence,
but for the call of an owl
and the one crack of a branch.

Yes, one raindrop of a word,
licking my naked lobe.

Tell, tongue to me,
the lacy streams in icy spring flood,
tracing the greening hills
of the valley's curves.

Yes, word, take off all your clothes.
Stand naked in whatever world exists
in the silence of our absence.

Tell me.

Some Days

Some days are like serving girls
rising and blowing out all the candles
in the house of the sky
then standing over the horizon and pouring
a lake of rose, a lake of blue
over the dark body of the sleeping mountains.

Other days sit on a curb muttering,
a wine bottle by their side.

So many days are as gray and alike
as insurance offices,
and we are lost in triplicate.

Days like crows
and we the dead men's eyes.
Unmendable, like God's rain,
they fall on both the just and unjust.
We can do nothing on those days.
Old before their dawn, they perch
on our pillows, and cackle,
"Don't bother getting up."

Send those days to the insurance office.
Don't believe them:
There are playful days that couch behind
the last curtains of night.
Leave out bowls of milk for them.
Let them catch you, let them purr and sit in your lap.

Days as bulging as over-ripe berries
and we, the celebrating robins.

Days of April daffodils
tooting yellow horns of foolish happiness,
and we follow, dancing, as if
all the days were one day
and our flesh, all the days of spring,
sugaring the newly-wed days summer,
for those of a swollen autumn.

Let Us Resume Our Conversation

Give a great shout
and startle the night so
that it rolls up the blackened
shutters of the day.

Oh sun, our first and brightest god.
Oh sky, floor of heaven.
Vagabond wind,
birds with air in your bones,
trees and bushes like knuckled fingers
grabbing at earth and sun,
ants in your highways and nests,
spiders in your secrets.
Flowers and bees in your love affairs.

Oh, soul.
Oh words, in your thousands,
streaming from your hives.
Oh, you lovely and lonely hearts.

Oh people, with your shards of memory,
your wounds, rainbows and tangles,
your yeses and noes.

Let us take our grand hubbub,
walk it through the day,
and, once again, greet the night,
as we, in our ones and twos,
subtract ourselves into the silence
of the stars.

Another Ark

Praise these microbiota:
they float on the currents of my movement,
blind, trusting, anemone-handed;

they feel for whispers
outside the doors of small things.

Bless these microorganisms
that live at the end—
the very tips—
of my fingers
in absolute trust
that I, their vessel,
will not yet founder,
that they will be husbanded enough.

Oh, trillions of creatures
on the inside and outside of me,
I will do what I can to keep us alive,
following this net of stars,

floating on the earth's fiery mantle,
I am your continent,
trying to bring us home to Pangaea.

And bless all the journeys I have undertaken,
whether fool's errands or not,
whether completed or not.

And bless all those who have loved me,
even for a night. May I be forgiven that
my passion cooled and I was rarely strong enough.

And bless all the ideas I have in my head.
I will you into words on a page
like Noah's dove into the world seeking signs of life.

For a Steward in the Merchant Marine

Conjugations

My father
did certain things
to my mother,
then to me
and because of this,
certain possibilities
that might have been
were not

and certain things
that might have gone
one way
went another
and other things
that wouldn't have been,
are,

and my mother
did certain things
that she may
or may not
have been fated
to do
and because she did,

again,
certain things
that could have been
in me,
weren't,
went another way
and thus,

by fate and happenstance,
I am.

First Flight

Will we crash?
Will our wings break on the mountain?
Can birds fly as fast as us?

These are some of the questions I ask
as we fly to see the man
my mother says is my father.

In his apartment on Capitol Hill,
on the first television I ever see,
the animated bubbles of cleanser
are like clouds, but singing,
as they go down the drain.

Then the man called my father comes in.
My mother says he sails across the sea
and has been away a long, long time.

He looks at me.
I think he is surprised,
but not in a good way.
Somehow, my being here isn't right.
She should have left me home.

Then they disappear—
I suppose, now, into the bedroom—
and I'm left with the singing clouds of bubbles
chasing dirt and grime down the drain.

She didn't know how to answer my question,
What will happen if we fall?

She should have said,
People crash all the time.
Sometimes their wings grow back.
Sometimes they don't, and then

you just don't fly.

Puzzle

Once, while my father was away at sea,
before they divorced,
my mother, my sister and I

sorted the straight-edged border pieces
and the four right-angled corners,
from the jumble of inner pieces,

then took the unconnected bits of red barn,
pecking hens, crowing cock, hand-shaped
leaves on the tree and pieces of a sleeping dog,
to hold, turn and examine in our hands.

In seven days, it was done,
except for one small bit of blue sky,
which we never did find.

We put the puzzle on its rickety table aside:
A small almost-perfect window of happiness,
to wait until my father came home.

The secret was to work together.
The secret was to hold a small piece,
believe it had a place in the whole,

wait until it formed,
then snap it where it belonged,

pretend that missing piece
was there.

For a Steward in the Merchant Marine

There was no pegboard hung in the basement
with the tools and skills of manhood
for you to give to me.

I remember your ship,
small as a toy in the distance,
but slowly looming
as it crawled towards home
on the broad belly of the Sound.

Then its immense hull gliding
to berth to tower and thrum
above us on Pier 41, my sister,
my mother, me and

you, all the way from Japan,
down the gangplank to see us.
We were all happy. But once
home, too soon, you
paced and prowled the house.
You were dangerous.

Not much more of you than this do I have,
except perhaps these eyes,
which are your eyes, when
they narrow and harden, looking for
a horizon so far away it may never be found.

What We Had in Our Hands

My father could not *not* sail
                and my mother
could not wait for a man
                    who was never home and I
                        could not *not* dream
of the names of the   faraway places
he sailed.
        Yokohama, Ketchikan and the
                  oceans in between.

I asked my mother, *Why*
      do you have to
go out with men,
          you've got me?
But I need another
kind of love, she said.
      A man's
kind
      of love.
You understand?
I didn't but
      still
nodded my head.

We moved
      from the gravel road
            with the blackberry bushes
                where I grew up
to a house on a busy street,
      two doors down
          from a bar where
             a girl could honky-
             tonk and find,
                you know,
a man's kind of love.

My father from the sea knocked on the door of the house where he did not live
and I,
with pieces of a balsa wood model
                sailing ship

in my hands
had
to let him in
    and watch
    as my father went
    to the blinds
        to look out on the street.
He saw a car parked outside and a couple inside.
From my room,
    I heard her footsteps on the porch.
       Then the door opening.
Then a shock of silence.

It happens all the time.
An explosion.
    Shouts,

        curses,

        a crash.
A knife
against
my mother's
throat.

I'll kill you, he said.
    Dare you, she replied.
        Don't, I
            shouted, *I've*
              called the police.
They're coming.
        Don't.
        I'm watching.
        Standing here.
        I'll see. My mother
smiled. My father,
    defeated,
        took the knife away.

I saw him,
    hands cuffed
        behind his back,
            out the door,
              taken away.
Ketchikan, Yokohama,

broken pieces in my hand. I
had to try,
somehow,
to put back together.

Bruised, I Guess

When I asked her why, the morning after,
she didn't know. "Grownups just do things sometimes—
Neurotic—Broken inside—Maybe a psychiatrist can fix them."

The night before, when
she didn't want to sleep with my dad,
she had him sleep with me.

She found me downstairs on the couch.
"Why are you down here?
Did anything happen?"

And I guess he was just a little bit mean
and it was the middle of the night
and he didn't have all his self-control.

He was asleep, dreaming, as was I,
and he thought, maybe, I was
one of the men on his ship in the merchant marine

and this was his chance to get back at my mom
and me, because I was her son, and she babied me.

The morning after, when she took me to school
and I asked why, why did she let—
bruised, I guess, I was—

bruised, not my body,
but bruised like that word
neurosis

and I told myself
when I grow up, I—
when I grow up—

Sailor at Sea

Leave the kids behind.
Throw the friends away.
Stuff the suitcase.
Wander the night.
Grab a wild fuck in the park.

Give up, quit, go away.
Let the kids have the memory
of this leaving, and
her story.

I look at your face.
There's me there,
less 20 years.
And your mother.

I got deals I traded for you.
And I have spent years at sea
thinking of you,
and do not know who you are.

I want to touch your cheek,
say something,
some word,
that I have tried,
that I have failed.

Men give up their children.
What can I say?
My tongue is stone.

My Gift

I was born into war. So was my father.
The enemy? For me, it was my father.
For him it was his.

I was thirteen when my father told me
how he saw his father knock his oldest brother to the floor.
When my uncle tried to get up, my grandfather
knocked him down again, and said,
You don't get up until I tell you.

He jabbed his finger at me, just like
my grandfather jabbed his at his sons.
Don't you ever get any ideas.

But my father's dead.
I do have an idea.
He can't stop me.
I'm going to rewrite my father.

Take away his shot glass, give him a cola.
I'll put a paper umbrella in it.
He'll be surprised, but he'll like it,
because I've given him a playful, feminine side.

We'll wrestle and he'll let me win.
He'll be good at baseball and throw balls with me.

When he comes home from the sea, he'll want to stay.
When he goes back to his ship, none of us will have bruises,
and we'll be sorry to see him go.

In the Revisions

Because I didn't know.

The cross-outs of words I didn't mean.
The I-take-it-backs,
hooks and all.

A do-over.
Make it better.
Find the sense.

To go back and pick up the thread
I missed or dropped,
follow it out of the maze I've made.

I can do it
more delicately
deliberately:

To hold a moment
before God and say,
This
is what I meant.

Summer Light, Seattle

Momma's Boy

A broken water wheel,
abandoned in its stony stream.

My aunt's and cousins' house.
We didn't have a house.

No father anymore.
Boys who teased me until I cried.
She didn't know how to father a boy.
Punch them in the nose, she said.
But I didn't know how.

Punch me, she said,
and held her pillow in front of her face.

A boy hits his own mother
in the face. I've never
done anything harder.

Broken Ice

My older cousins and their friends dared the ice.
They jumped up and down.
"Break the ice, break the ice."

I could hear it cracking, like some under-the-ice animal,
burrowing towards us from under the bridge.
Felt it tunneling beneath my feet.

We all ran screaming for the bank.
But the bank was too high and
I couldn't get up by myself

and them damn kids, my cousin
with them, wouldn't help me.
But on the other side of the bridge,

the bank was low enough
for me to get up and
there would be no jeering faces.

But beneath the bridge, with every step,
the ice feathered with frost-white cracks
and water pooled around my unlaced shoes.

I had to fold myself down to my hands and knees,
crawl, touch my hands to the ice,
as if it were a sleeping body.

Crack lines, like little fish escaping,
wiggled across the ice.
It groaned as I crawled.

Right under my face, a small crack and
the black and sparkle of the stream underneath.
The plates of ice on which I crawled began to sink.

When I climbed to the top of the bank,
my cousins and their friends cheered,
glad I'd made it. But I walked right on by.

I learned,
even as the ice was crackling,
I didn't need anybody.

Blackberries

I put on my winter clothes in summer:
Jacket and flannel hat but,
so I could pluck and feel,
I wore no mittens.

In the tangled bushes, there is always a way in.
For shy creatures close to the ground,
a hole in the brambles.
And if, on hands and knees, working
first one shoulder through, then the other,

I too would be a small furred animal
hidden in the stickered green where
the roots of things, thick stalked and studded
with hard brown thorns, came out of the ground.

Entwined in scent of ripening berries,
the cool earth beneath my belly,
the flutter of wings in the leaves above
my flanneled head. The neighborhood sounds

far away.

Momma's Henchmen

I

Thrown out again.
We thought we'd find
a hideaway.
But all my sister and I got
was another one of Momma's dens.
My life's that way.
I'd been there before.

An innocent enough looking place,
We hid in the bedroom section of a department store.
In through the skylight.
We thought we'd fool 'em.
But there they were.
Momma's bodyguards,
hiding in the curtains
behind the beds.

We ran, but
there was one we couldn't shake,
even when we got outside.
There he was.
Cool,
taking a smoke in the alley,
nonchalant.

Waiting to beat us up.
Not this time
We got him from behind
in a choke hold,
then busted his arm.

II

We thought we got away.
Ran alleyways under
the black stitchings of
fire-escapes,
garbage trucks like elephants

screaming and lifting dumpsters
with their metal tusks.

Finally, the backstairs of my apartment,
sneak through the window.
Damn! Gangsters again.
Like dogs laying on my sofa,
owning my refrigerator.
Just waiting.
They knew we had to come.

III

They'll do more than
just hurt us a little, I said.
They'll teach us a lesson.

Fuck 'em, my sister said.
She was going to rip off some ears.
I stopped her.
Momma's henchmen will take you upstairs.

Then, I thought I could hear momma's laughter
from deep inside.
Momma. Stop it, I shouted.
Leave us alone.

IV

I know momma's smiling.
She's got so many henchmen in her pay.
My life's that way. That's the way things are.

Bleeder

We were two junior high nobodies
squared off
in a stand of scraggly pines.

We even drew a crowd,
like with Billy Chellas.
Billy was bad. Fought his way
to the Top 10, but no further
He was a bleeder.

We didn't want to fight,
but we got started and
I could hit him whenever I wanted.
I remember his face, sad
like a dog left out in the weather.

His fists useless,
squeezed tight in front of his face,
mine flew like birds.

The crowd of suck-asses
could feel I was going to win.
Yelled for his blood.
"Hit him again."
They didn't know his name.

Blood from his nose,
and one eye swelled shut.
If I won,
his friend, Norman Bartley,
would be next.
Then Billy Chellas, then…

I put down my fists.

Debut

The stage:
Holly Park Lanes parking lot
Libations: stolen wine and beer
from the nearby Safeway
The audience:
Just the eyes of the stars
—He toasted them—
and his two or three friends
—He toasted them—
and the 30-year old waitress
Kathy in Al's diner
where he washed dishes
one dollar an hour
and French dip au jus
—with fries—
in the restaurant booth

where a girl
whose name
disappeared
on a scrap of paper
said   she liked
a little dark meat
every now and then and
he giggled—he knew
what she meant—

it took six months
for him and the girl
to get together
both so wasted
that last night
that zippers, hooks
and penis too
wouldn't work
while Connie Frances
sang "I'm Sorry"
—for all that didn't happen
and of course all that did—
on that last night

the night before the
Army took him
—and Vic who was
with him that night
in the parking lot
beneath black
and starry sky
—whose name
twenty years later
was inscribed
on the black wall memorial
and the wheels
of the constellations
look like they haven't moved
since they slipped a sliver
of a parsec
when
he surprised them both
when he still a boy
kissed Kathy the woman
in the parking lot
outside Holly Park Lanes.

1958

began with Sputnik falling out of the sky.
                              It missed me,
but ten days earlier my mother
        on Christmas Eve went back to her
                        ex-con boyfriend,
Red.

                                        She
was just married to Bob
            who the Army had shipped
to Korea in September,
            two months before I turned fifteen.
I really liked him a lot
            and was ready
                    to make him my father.
                    But she said, *Red*
shouldn't be alone on Christmas.
                    And,
                    Nothing's

                                    going to happen,

She was my mom.
                What could I say?
                        But not too many days
after Sputnik fell to earth, it hit me:
                She stayed out all night
and came home with Red, who
                        smashed my face until
                I quit calling her,
Whore.

In February, Pope Pius XII,
        my pope, who looked down on me
from the classroom wall,
declared Saint Claire
                to be the patron saint
                        of television
because when
        she was too sick
                to leave her sick bed,
                        she saw
and heard
        the Holy Mass on

                    her bedroom wall.
On my wall,
                as I waited for my mother
                        to come home,
I saw headlights
like spun-glass spiders
                crawl and fade.

The hula hoop,
                bright and red and gyrating
like an errant ring of Saturn
                            around the Seafair Queen's waist,
was in July and
        by then I had long ago quit living
—from January to June—
                when my mother said,
"OK, we'll leave."

We moved to California. I was popular. Guys
            chose me to be on their team.
But then,
        for ten days,
shortly after
the date Wikipedia gives
for the beginning
of the Great Chinese Famine,
        for ten days,
she didn't come home.

Until my 16th birthday.

She took us from her
            sister and mother
                    and our cousins
                            and put us in the car
back to Seattle.
        But the car threw a rod
in Portland and Red
            had to come and rescue us.

A month and a half later, on the last day of the year,
Che Guevara and Fidel Castro liberated Havana.
My Sierra Madre was still in the future.

Partly Heliotropic

The man my mother chose for her destruction,
who beat me until I showed some sign of surrender,
the ex-con who was locked in a closet as a boy
and, as a man, robbed a Safeway then
locked the grocers in the freezer,

once asked me in our kitchen in Holly Park,
the beer bottle in his hand stabbing at the air,
Who's the smartest man in the whole world?

I shrugged. Nobody I knew.
Then he and his ex-con friend argued:
Socrates. Diogenes.
Both having some appeal
to men who had been kept in cages.

Socrates: People think they're smart, but they're not.
Diogenes: Carried a lantern looking for an honest man,
spent most of his life naked.

I don't know who won the argument.
But after I left home and joined the Army,
I saw Socrates' name
on a paperback book in the PX.
I had to give it a try.

Back in the barracks in the top bunk.
I cried as the turning pages led me out
from the darkness of caves up to the sun.
So many shadows: my mother and Red,
me and my sister, flickering on a stone wall.

Often and without warning,
I find myself a shadow again,
like reluctant wallpaper
trying to unpeel myself.
Caves, then sun, all the
dreamy ways I've used
to come back up.

Partly heliotropic, I'm grateful
to Socrates and Diogenes.
All those who briefly stood
with whatever lantern or stub of candle they had
through the generations like fireflies
blossoming in a field
before falling into their darkness.

Naked in the marketplace,
shivering in a freezer,
locked in a hole in Walla Walla,
tucked under an arm,
face bashed, nose broke.

A mother in a dark bedroom
pulling him into her
to save him, to save her,
for a moment,
incandescence,
then the darkness
and our shadows flickering
on a stone wall.

Forgiveness

Now, many years later,
I stop the car and listen
to the small crinkly sounds
the engine makes
as it cools in the fog.
It could have been here,
by these dunes.

I don't know what happened.
Maybe there was a smell.
He just jumped.

Could he have survived?
And did he stand on shaky legs
waiting for us to return?

My mother and her boyfriend,
in a fog of alcohol, drove on.

Now in the distance,
the shaggy white surf
paws at the land.
I let all the windows down
and the night come in.
Start the car, drive slow.

Not looking in the backseat,
I can feel the night's
black nose,
cold and wet,
pushing against my neck.

The Flags of My Allegiance

Yesterday, her arms to the elbow
in the Kenmore,

I helped her draw the clothes,
sopping wet,
through the wringer.
My shirts and pants, and her dresses
flopping on the line.

Take me by the shoulders,
dip me, scrub me in soapy water
draw my soul out
in long and fine chanted words
then leave me well-scrubbed and clean all over,
in breezes of blackberry
and lilac, fluttering on the line
—a free verse again—

A shirt, a skirt, her satin slip,
the snowy sheets of my mother's bed.

Summer Light, Seattle

Green blackberries with their sour fingers
pulled at my tongue and wouldn't let go.

All summer I'd watched them bake,
turn cherry, slowly blacken.

Each berry, a basket of sweet salmon eggs
swollen from the long buzzing days.

In the dusk, as the crickets jingled their spurs,
we played kick-the-can

and I was the one
they couldn't find.

Red ants, big as my thumb.
They would eat me alive, my cousins said.

Then, light like melon flesh
spilled from our open door

as my mother called my name.

French Press

I wait for the grounds
of the French press to settle.
The barista plays something old
by Ella Fitzgerald.
The same songs she sang
on the radio one morning
while I watched dark drops
fall into the glass percolator,
slowly staining its
clear water black.

This is our first breakfast
since my father
went back to sea
and my mother
wears her apron
with bright red apples
falling from a bowl
and does a jitterbug
as she stirs our oatmeal and
scats with Ella on the radio,
"Always True to You
in my Fashion."

Afterwards, I will take
the milk bottles out
to the metal crate
on the porch.
For some reason
I am happy,
even though she will soon
begin looking for a house
without my father.

The grounds have settled,
the coffee in the glass press
is black as obsidian.
The barista plays
"I Won't Dance,"
yet if we were in
that kitchen again,
I would, just ask me.

Love letter then,

The Coupe de Ville and the Burro

After tipping the bellhop,
I stand with my bag in the portico.

At the front of the line, a Cadillac,
then a woodie, a Sex Wax decal in the window.

There is even a buckboard
—sacks of flour in its box.

But waiting for me is a sad-eyed burro,
who does not want to move.

That's the way it is with burros,
unless you give them the whip,

and we've both had enough of that.

Plants in Tough Places

I always want to cheer
when I see
a twig with leaves like wings
ledged on the pockmarked
face of a cliff,
as if in a lady's flower box.

Trembling,
it can't help
its slow leap
into gravity's wind.

So what
if God's chisel
is always chipping
at its stony holdfast?

What have odds
ever had to do with it?

Wild and Windy Day

The waves, like an angry crowd,
overleapt themselves,
trying for a shot at the sandy shore.

The small pond by the side of the road
took its chance and ran for it,
overflowed wherever it could.

The gulls screamed, opened
their wings, clawed their way
up the storm walls of the wind.

The rain began to fall,
beating at all things with
small furies of cold-hard fists.

The wind shuddered my parked car,
wild waters leapt in the air `
and I, as best as I could, joined them.

Elliptical

Oh frog, I've been sick and not wanted to get out of bed.
Oh frog, I've been blue and not had one worthwhile thought.

Six months ago, our planet ellipsed full gear into summer,
your pond dried up and you, green-bean green
beneath the drying mud, went to sleep.

Now half an orbit on, in this slow and cold half of the year,
oh frog, at four in the morning in the December dark,
your nocturnal celebration announces your return.

Welcome back. I've almost forgotten how you cheer up the rain,
your little sound, zipping and unzipping your small cloth of night.

Hills Gathered Around Hecker Pass

As day breaks, fog from the pine-backed ridges
spills down the bristled slopes,
and swatches of darkness,
caught in the pine needles of knuckled
branches, slowly fade.

These dark and quilled hills,
filling and brimming with light,
could continue their sleep
or, like great bison, wake

and get up and amble down
to the last twinkling lights
of Watsonville

where, sleepy-eyed,
we too would wake,
and remember the lives we left in the hills
so long ago.

They would kneel down for us
and take us back.

The Meeting

At the edge of the pasture,
a trail curves along the
knuckled toes of the foothills
while horses graze below.

I am happy to be a small thing
between the rocky *morro* above
and the young grass
where these horses wander.

From a distance,
they are tiny, plastic,
the horses I played with as a boy.

Geldings and mares
browse at the grass,
their tails flick and swish.

Two foals
tear through the herd.

I walk closer.
A few elders look up.
I tell them I
come in peace.

I step softly,
like a father
checking in on his
sleeping children,
then stop to
look at the chestnut foal:
a short bristly black mane,
a wisp of a black tail.

She's curious,
walks through the herd
on careful, delicate steps,
looking directly at me.

She stops,
approaches
like a girl
at her first dance.

She has emerged and
I stand where I am and
we bring our faces together,
my small nose touching
the large, soft muffin of hers.

I caress her flickering ear,
rub the bristle of her mane,
thump her haunch and reach under
to run my hand along
her smooth, nippled belly.

She tosses her head.
I walk into the herd.
I can feel her behind me,
walking with me.

Moon-Called

All I could do was watch
even as crickets sang
and even as the moon began
to bloom from the darkness.

We had driven our cars to the top of Loma Prieta
to come as close as we could to the full eclipse
like metal filings pulled heavenward.

On both sides of the narrow twisting road
between the cliff face and cliff edge,
we parked our cars
got out
looked up
pointed.

In the narrow one-way channel hundreds of people
and still cars kept bumping in, like platelets
squeezing through a capillary tunnel.
Moon-called
to go as high as we could.

The eclipse took so long
that some turned their cars around
headed back
even as the latecomers kept coming:
they met head-on—hood nosed against hood.

Drivers with stallion horsepower
stuck their small heads out their windows
shouted and shook fists.

That's when the deer in me wanted to run.
But all I could do was watch.
War! We can't get away from it.

The stars so close
so bright.
We atop the mountain
touching the sky.

The crickets' sound
the sound starlight makes
as it breaks on our rounded shore.

Bryce Canyon

Hoodoo formations
red and gray monks
surpliced with snow.

Stone gardens
cloistered by horizon
and canyon walls.

The stillness of bones
and the quiet of sky.

I can take off the clothes
of being human here
the very flesh of it.

how is it

the small-fisted buds
on the maple trees
uncurl themselves
against the sky

small
green fingers

turn
the huge page
of the season

silently turn
this granite mountain
from winter to spring

On Making it to the Moon

This blue planet is not out there
not floating on the cover of
the *Whole Earth Catalog*,
nor is it a dominion claiming corporate logo.

It's in here, from the bulge of Africa
       back again to the bulge of Africa
carried in our gut, in the palms of our hands,
       in the light in our eyes

and, at this moment, it's all the crowned heads
       of our grandchildren.
emerging from the birth canal.

It's in here, in our blood, and it is dying.

It is

a blessing to lie
on your moist, green ground,
to feel your body press against mine
as you show me to the sun,

to feel your breasts
graze my face,
to feel your breath—
the air in your sky—
flow into my lungs.

To slip my fingers through
your silky, spiky grass
and burrow them into
your wet earth.

I want to come home
and celebrate you
with the exaltation of mountains
and the quietude of cowslips and daisies.

How could I
have forgotten you;
how could I leave you
when you're always here?

Let me be a fish in your stream,
an owl in your oak
and the rabbit in its talons;
a lichen-stained stone
beside your sacred well,
or a man,
here in the grass
at your shrine.

Love letter then,

as one might write
from a homeless camp

to I don't know who
with a stub of pencil
and a scrap
about some shimmering
a splash of moon
found in the most unlikely

and I just wanted to tell you
about that time
night
cold
my breath in plumes

nobody
nobody else
not even the thought of you
but I saved it

the memory of wind in trees
like a highway far away
that this
I don't know what
a handful of ash and spark
might be

and did I say I missed you
in the spaces in between?

Safety

Two deer caught in my lights.
The fawn so small, it could have been born today.

I braked in time, and the doe
scrambled up the steep berm
into the woods, and the fawn ran
on tottering steps on the hard ribbon
of the mountain road to another pair
of headlights, coming towards us.

The other car swerved and stopped
and we in our separate cars
watched the fawn walk gingerly over the asphalt
until it came to a place
where the berm was more gentle
and not so steep
and where it disappeared into the woods.

We rolled down our windows.
We were happy we were slow.
Hoped it would find its mother.

Then she drove off and I waited
and saw the doe come out of the dark,
following, I imagined, the scent of its fawn.

The road was dark, and far from anyone.
She was a woman and I a man.
But, today, it didn't matter.

Cricket Lover

The crickets on my lawn
each with a wild violin
played in mad ululation.

It made no difference that I lacked
a left or a right forewing.
I went outside and bent my knee.

Brushed my two forearms together
and began to play.
Then my love came outside,

knelt in the grass,
picked me up in her hand,
cupped me to her ear

and took me to her bed.

Kilcatherine Remains

An old, end-of-the-world
sadness
hangs over me.

So many ruins—
eaten by lichen and rain
—my heart breaks.

This old graveyard, littered
with fallen tombstones,
the names on their surfaces
erased by the drifting
of centuries across their faces.

The church's stone roof
tumbled to ground long ago.
The window's empty iris
on one of its remaining walls
still holds its bit of sky.

Now, as the all the oligarchs
squeeze the last drops of blood
from all the rocks of
all the times before ours,

I will embrace the lumpy,
anvil-shaped goddess
turned-to-a-boulder
overlooking Balleycrovane Harbor

and inside megalithic circles,
dance with the dancers
of vanished millennia
under the moonlight.

Escrow

One-hundred and twenty times we signed,
sutured our names in cursive to each other

as we did escrow and I got turned on
like a teenager doing a slow-dance.

I wanted to squeeze you to me,
reach out and grab handfuls

of your dirt and stones.
Daub myself all over

with the mud of you,
as though tattooed—a quarter acre,

a house, dog, oak and apple trees
—but with ink that was less than permanent.

One Good Day

Yesterday I made eight thousand dollars, Ray Carver.
Eight thousand bucks in one day.
Like good bread, warm from the oven,
cut with a knife.

I don't know what life's all about, Ray,
except moments of satisfaction like a bird
on top of a pine sings to the sky,
then disappears.

Ray Carver, we are uncomfortable with men
but love women.

I got off on the wrong foot, of that I'm sure.
I could have been a king—I was—
but my cousins and the boys down the street
were jealous and did their best to kidnap me,
wrap me in a blanket, poke me with sharp sticks.
—They were angels when my mother came home.

Ray, I made eight thousand dollars yesterday.
—I could have ordered the finest wine
and called room service.

A Lesser Heaven

I have worked all my life
to go to the Federal Office Building
and apply for Social Security

The woman there was kindly, as if she knew
darkness and rain might be coming on
and I had traveled a long way.

She held her door open, showed me a chair, read a statement,
then asked if I would initial and affirm all that I said was so, was so.
It was, and I did.

Every year I worked, more than 50 years, on one sheet of paper.
The first answered ad: One dollar an hour plus a bologna sandwich for lunch
to weed an old man's garden.

The bank where I never balanced,
two dollars short, twenty-five cents on a good day.
Let go with a baby on the way.

Stacking ladders in a hundred degrees
in a freight car in a ladder factory
where the little guy I worked with
didn't like the way I talked and
kept asking me to suck his cock, "Hey, hey."
With a baby on the way.

A decade later, stacking cans in a cannery.
A decade later, stacking numbers in a database.
Twenty or so jobs at such and such an hour and so much a year,
made right, stacked peacefully in a column on the paper in her office.

And the questions, how long I was married and to whom,
as if the spaces for the names of all my wives
and the place where we married were little empty beds
where, one by one, all the years of my life were coming home.

Autumnal Road

I still stop when I pass San Miguel.
Of course, you aren't there,
where the motel once was
under the laurels near the road
that wandered in
from the pale summer hills.

I came to your door
and my ears flickered
with what you whispered,
and lust slid all along my limbs,
like a shivering sleeve.

We made love all week
and I began to think of marriage.
We drove back, that last time, to Camp Roberts
and in the dark your fingers touched and played with me.

Would you have said yes
and if you had, what road
would you and I be wandering now?

Another Flower

We slap boxed down the aisle
between the two rows of bunk beds.
He had springs in his feet. He
darted and feinted and jabbed. He,
lithe as the wind in the trees.
He, the tide rolling and surging
through the rocks on the shore.
"Come on, come and get me," he chanted.
Me, I plodded and waited, but when he came at me,
I caught his music and I danced and pranced too.

GI's then, even friends and buddies,
called each other by their last name.
But I called him Cicero.
In the car, when we were on patrol,
he was quiet and thoughtful,
his laugh, soft and rumbly, like far away thunder.
When I said there had to be a God, a first cause,
his Socratic "Why?" rippled with bemusement.
He was easy to spend a shift with.

After my enlistment was up,
he came to see me at my aunt's.
I think my grandmother fixed us dinner.
Then we watched TV and went to bed
and, sometime in the night,
he lightly placed his hand on me and I,
I removed it, not quickly, but gently,
like asking a butterfly to go to another flower.

Bradley, Population 128

Empty as a bottle tossed
on the cracked, buckled highway.

The auto shop's siding
has popped most of its nails.

An old rag of a dog
sleeps under the oak.

Lace curtains grayed by the years
wave from the half-open window of the house

where a tumbleweed leans
patiently against the door, waiting.

The boarded-up cafe where
the pretty young waitress worked.

She married the kid stationed at Camp Roberts:
Abbott, from Texas.

In a blue niche in the tower
of the white church,

Our Lady of Guadalupe,
Madonna still cradles her child.

The young man who once stayed
a few nights with a friend of the bride?

Fifty years later, looking at the
gray-ribbed Nacimiento River bridge—

—just passing through.

In Newgrange

I stood in darkness swallowed
as in a womb.

One with it:
Deep, India ink black.

Then, from a projector,
the winter solstice sun.

Light like a cloud
of spermatozoa spilling
down the corridor of darkness.

For seventeen minutes, according to the guide.
I saw light   dance the dance of life

deep under the tumulus as sun and time advanced
and zippered it

back again
into the night.

My eyes loved the dance of light
but it's the dark my heart knows is home.

Old Man's Love Song

Though stepping out of the shower,
we see each other naked,

and, while sleeping,
we twist around as promiscuous
as clothes in a washtub,

in the everydayness of everyday life,
we don't see one another.

What happened to our wild lusts?
We were savage for each other.

How did we become captives,
chained to our well-ordered hours:
the made beds, folded clothes,
paychecks, mortgage payments
and even the posting
of pictures of grandchildren
on the refrigerator door?

Don't get me wrong,
I wouldn't trade what we've built,
the sweetness of these days,
even for a night with a wild woman
who would set fire to my blood
and make me feel young,

unless she was you.

Lost

The wandering mind sends out flares
and sparks of meaning no one understands.
This is where the war with gravity ends.
The lithe and strong, now bent and frail,
shuffle in walkers or sit in wheelchairs.

Here in the midst of this, by the floral chair,
stands my aunt. She takes me to her room.
She wants to make me coffee. But there is none.
Would I like a Tootsie Roll? Of course.
Then I give her the present I found at the stationer's.
A blue-breasted bird, made of plush.

I ask, how are they, the dead?
She wants her mother, my grandmother,
to buy her the house in Santa Clara— again.
The one she lived in for fifty years.
Maybe her sister, my mother,
twenty years dead, will move in with her.

She tells me, Jimmy has taken up
with his brother Donny's wife.
Billy, her youngest,
is back on the bottle and run off
with Dot, my aunt's best friend.

Fifteen minutes is the most I can take.
She waves as I walk away.
Perhaps she understands.
The blue-breasted bird I brought for her
now sits on the windowsill, watching
those still capable of flight as they land on the oaks.

Dad died, she said. *Last weekend.*
He just fell over and died.
I don't know how I'm going to tell mother.
But mother's going to take me home.
She's going to take me home.

Balloons

Ninety years old, Great-grandchildren
played on the floor by his feet.
Above his head,
colored balloons dangled strings
and bounced along the ceiling.
One drifted down to his chair
and when he put out his palm,
the balloon stopped falling
and stood on its dangled string,
as if it were growing
from his outstretched hand.
And he talked to it,
"You need some help,"
Then he asked for a scissors,
cut its string and
watched it rise.

Next morning,
in that small breath of air
that came in from under
the closed door to his room,
all the balloons were bouncing on the floor,
towing their strings, as if swimming:

small little bounces,
tiny heartbeats,
really.

Old Address Book

It was under a worn-out sock in the back of the drawer:
a cracked cover of black vinyl and paper
thin as the skin on the back of an old man's hand.

For those who had moved,
the addresses and phone numbers were scratched out.
But for the dead and missing,
I kept the numbers of their houses and phones,
as if those paths to their former existence
were not addresses to nowhere.

The newly dead,
those who have died in this paperless time,
I keep in a special section—
dead—in my electronic phone book.

I know I can't call, or text, or,
not ever again,
sit across from him at the table
as we eat spaghetti at *Restauranti Italiano*

and hear him shout, his face
as red as the Chianti we drink
as he tells me once more about
his first nude encounter group.

In my brain, like some unexcavated Troy,
there's a whole city of the dead and forgotten
—more foolish and beautiful than ever.

They don't go away.
They just get covered up,
not by dirt,
but by the first day without them
and the next
and next.

Disconnected

After "Message to a Former Friend" by Tony Hoagland

I want to call you,
but you are fifty years away,
if not gone: a distance
time can no longer measure.

Remember when we'd say goodbye?
You'd call out *Go well,*
and I'd reply, *Stay well?*

I want to hire a skywriter
to tattoo *Stay well*
across the evening's belly
so you know I am alive.

Remember when you wrote a poem
inspired by Robert Bly,
and sent it to him,
and he wrote you back?

I didn't know if I had talent,
but I knew you did.
I learned how to be a poet from you.

I'm sorry. I was an arrogant ass.
I thought I knew better than you.
I thought I knew how you should live your life.

Did you ever return to the shore?
If you did,
did you dip your face
in the sea once again;
longing madly for God?

Michigan

The quiet guy,
who sat at the back of the workshop,
came down the path
and stood by the steps to the cabin's porch
where I sat after breakfast,
lazy as a fly on a hot day.

You never know with strangers.
Most of the time,
I'm on my guard.
But not that day.

All the man wanted was to look at the view,
for a moment, before he left.
Maybe feel the morning air,
and then to say
he was from Michigan.

It's something we like to do.
Stand next to someone
and say,
I'm from there.

Anywhere.

And for someone to say,
Really?
All that way!

And then agree,
Sure is pretty here.

Yes, sure is.
Have a nice

nice talking to you.

That's all he wanted.
To say he was from Michigan.

On the Amtrak

Divorced for the third time,
I no longer like the woman I loved
just a year ago,

although, when I came home yesterday
with good news from the cardiologist,
my heart still ached for her.

Late in life, still learning to be with people.
It's safe to smile and, I think,
they like to smile back.

And dying alone, perhaps,
is no different
than sleeping alone.

Cars in front yards sleep the sleep of rust
in slow procession out my window.

Sophisticated

I used to be sophisticated with a girl on a date at the movie.
Sophisticated, I would drape my left arm along the back of her seat
    and, with my right, offer her my bag of popcorn.
Sophisticated, from the back of her seat, I was so suave, to the top of her shoulder,
    my hand was as soft as a falling leaf.
Sophisticated, more popcorn, my right hand offered a diversion.
Sophisticated, you know where this is going and, of course, so did she.
Gauche, top of the shoulder was about as far as I had the courage to go.
Brave shoulder, my arm was falling asleep.
Impatient, she grabbed fistfuls of popcorn from my sack.
More recently, as a newly single old man,
Sophisticated again, I waited next to the trendy mushrooms
    in the produce section.
Sophisticated, looking lost, in a little boy sort of way.
Sophisticated, *Please ma'am,* I hold out a button mushroom,
    what do you do with these?

Does the Road

I will leave behind

so many selves like snakeskins:
a blue baby jumper with a sailboat on its chest,
beached and left on the floor when I stood up,
slapped my thigh and cantered
through the chaparral canyons
like a miniature Gene Autry,

whose cap guns I, in turn,
traded for an M1 and fatigues,
which were shed for tailored shirts
that showed off my muscles,
then the wedding suit—now covered with dust
and half-slipped from its hanger in the closet.

Even my skin hangs loose. My wife
says I look fine, but I know looks fade.
These are the last miles. These old telomeres,
like bald tires, won't go much further.
What do I do with what's left?

Just yesterday, these shinbones
climbed Cerro San Luis, strode the Cuesta Ridge.
After the walker, the wheelchair, the box
how do I thank them?
Stand them out by the young elm,
let them be wrapped in bougainvillea?

When Jack Kennedy got America
into track suits and running,
my thighs, with a million others, ran too.
When I was six, these feet ran so fast
they forgot to touch the ground.

Didn't these hip and pelvic bones
love to gallop across the meadows of my day?
Don't they still answer when they hear
your soft whinny from across the room?

I know what I'll do with this grief:
bury it beneath a papaya tree.
Two hundred years from now,

it will be wrapped into the roots,
turned to sweetness.

I will this worshipful tongue—
still learning to pray—
to the river, the delta
where it touches the sea.

These eyes, (how hungry they've been,)
in love with skies and faces, flips of hair,
the curves of a woman's body,
where can I put them?
My skull? My clouds of wondering?

I'll tell my wife
to leave them on the porch railing,
toward the sun slipping into the Santa Lucia,
oh simple mountain range,
oh patron saint of the blind.

What We Hold

Only echoes.

Even my face is not mine,
it's theirs, my parents,
and before them, their parents,
and so on.

My voice, its very timbre, theirs.

This scrawl, blown like a spider's line across the page, theirs.

These scarred fingers that squeeze my throat
to keep its sadness locked inside,
they are as much theirs as mine.

And these men who rule the world, who send the tanks
that break down our doors, they are my father.

Long ago, I met him on a dark crossroad.
We were both frightened.
We had swords and
neither of us knew who the other really was.

And when my wife and I hold each other in the night,
all the lovers who ever loved hold us,
and we must hold them, too.

Inalienable

If you ignore their faces,
they look like you and me--
these deplorables, these riffraff
with their fingers hooked in
mesh of the cages
we put them, shoulder
to shoulder, standing room only.

They look like average
Americans standing, waiting
for the light to change
in New York City. Without
their faces, they can be you
or me, or our children, our

toddlers hiding under crumpled
aluminum foil blankets
because times are
different now and we
have to protect our country
from people we don't

want to know
look like us.

Treasure

You are already in the mine.
What you need is
whatever lamp you can find.

Take the pickax of your desperation.
Dig the memories marbled
with the fossils of trilobites
and the black songs of the boughs
of trees fallen ages ago.

They have slept long enough.
Load them in the cart

and take them back up above,
so that they may sing
their black veined songs in
the sunlight once again.

Does the Road

Does the road you walked on long ago remember you?
Do its pebbles recall the space between your toes that they clung to?
Do the hills look over their shoulders and whisper as you walk by?

You were as happy as a leaf on an oak on a hillside,
beside a pond where one lone frog sang in the night.
And there was a door where glad voices greeted you
        when you walked in.

That road, those pebbles and those hills
with the leaf and the oak and the frog song and the pond
        and the glad voices,
they walk along with you now
        and they are as lost and fading as you or me.

The Wooden Box My Father Brought Back from Japan

Painted on its lid,
two snowy egrets in the sky,
three puffy clouds,
green reeds in a blue pool.

In the middle of the side panel,
an invisible horizontal slat.
If slid just a half an inch,
it frees the whole panel
for its next small move.

After all the moves,
a small drawer on the side,
chiming as I pull it open.

I had forgotten about this.
It's not the treasure in secret places,
but that there are secret places,

and sometimes a lover or a poet,
with fingers of intuition,
can touch my breastbone
and suddenly singing spills out,
a musical place I had forgotten
opens in my body.

Road's End

Along the cut of the old logging road,
seedlings of pine crowd the lane.

Its washboarded, gullied surface
gives out, melts into the ground,
and becomes a trail.

A wandering trail
for hoof print of deer
paw print of cougar.

In the newly-risen
full-moon night,
I have no place to go.

Two moon-drunk moths
flutter above,
show me the way.

Roots grow from my toes,
my arms lift to the sky
and my pine-needle hands

gather the stars.

Writing Place

The weeds are knee high down the hill
to the place where I plan to write.
It's under the oak, with a mid-day splash

of sun and a view to the valley.
I'll put in a wood stove for the rain and the cold,
buy a desk and with pen in my hand,

watch the gray tailed squirrel
climb stutter-step
the trunk of the oak.

It's taken a lifetime to get here and never a straight line,
but as I rest against the mower and look back
through these high green weeds,

it's a lovely swathe I've cut
to the door of the place I want to go.

Acknowledgments

Alaska Quarterly Review: "Forgiveness"
Blue Unicorn: "The Flags of My Allegiance"
Cathexis Northwest Press: "French Press, "If a Fish," "It is," "Reflections"
The Comstock Review: "Does the Road," "Moon-Called," "One Good Day"
DMQ Review: "how is it"
Robinson Jeffers Tor House Foundation 2004 Poetry Prize: "Partly Heliotropic"
Sarasota Review: "Autumnal Road"
White Pelican: "Love letter then,"

Special thanks to the wonderful teachers over the years who kindled the flame of
poetry in my brain:

Ellen Bass, Robert Bly, Galway Kinnell, Phyllis Koestenbaum, Edward Small-
field, Sally Ashton, Jeffrey Levine, Rachel Kann, Edward Hirsch, Rick Bursky,
Brendan Constanine, Kimberly Grey, Courtney Kampa, Elena Karnia Bryne,
my sister, Pat Burns, who lived in the same pain-crazed family as me, but as a girl
in a much more patriarchal time, and to Rosie Wolf whose love and support is
my refuge and delight.

Also Available
from
Cathexis Northwest Press:

Something To Cry About
by Robert Krantz

Suburban Hermeneutics
by Ian Cappelli

God's Love Is Very Busy
by David Seung

that one time we were almost people
by Christian Czaniecki

Fever Dream/Take Heart
by Valyntina Grenier

The Book of Night & Waking
by Clif Mason

Dead Birds of New Zealand
by Christian Czaniecki

The Weathering of Igneous Rockforms in High-Altitude Riparian Environments
by John Belk

How to Draw a Blank
by Collin Van Son

En Route
by Jesse Wolfe

Cathexis Northwest Press

CPSIA information can be obtained
at www.ICGtesting.com
Printed in the USA
LVHW050913030621
689238LV00018B/768